I AM A POET

THERE IS NOTHING YOU CAN DO TO STOP ME!!

ANUSTHA PAL

Contents

Contents

Foreword

the author of this book is Ms Anustha Pal, started her work from the age of nineteen.

she was taking graduation, at that she learn and discover herself as a amazing poet.

she continue her work after that. this book is written on the ending of her graduation.

Scars, Door to my soul, Aiepathy, Anustha diary, under my umbrella and flashbacks in my

casette are the previous books that she have written.

Preface

this book is collection of wonderful poetry of world in the form of words.

it is joy to read this poetry cause the expression and catchy words are used here which attract you read.

the writings holding the feelings which are like different colors of rainbow.

something that is relaxing and make you feel calm.

this book has tittle "i am poet" cause this time i want to express what this writing an poems meant to me.

cause they are priceless and i felt them as my one of the biggest acheivment.

i want that nobody can never able to interupt me from writing that is big goal

for me chase. so for my own acknowledgment i have written this book.

1. Through my window

Through my window,
I can see the bright world having
Dirt on their shirt.
The heavenly woods with the raining
Clouds,
The honeysuckle covered by
dry leaves of Colour brown.
I can see how days turn into months,
And months into year,
How these days treat you like a warm
Blanket of care.
How the life goes on in the simplicity of
Smitten hearts,
How smile turn into a mirth jar.
How the dawn blanks our hearts,
The twilight holding the strings of guitar.
The quartet swinging and smashing the
Songs and rhymes,
How the chivalrous soul blossoms the life.
Through my window I have seen the baby
Pups hiding in the canal.
How they grow in time spends.
I see breeze touching the canopy,
I feel ecstasy than ever.

I also have seen how the life change the lives,
Your happiness may be someone else reason
Of happiness and winkles in their life.
This window opens the door of beautiful life.

2. Garden

Trespasser in my garden,
Come and go.
My garden is not for the community
Still, they make me feel so.
Some started loving my flowers
Some just pluck them,
some make me feel more than I can
and some make this garden hell.
My flowers, my weeds, my plants and
My tress, even the fence that clings
can feel,
The things that I don't want to reveal.
The trophy of beauty is a wound,
Over this garden, I spend a precious amount.
They have and have not worried about my falcons,
There in the orchards, there are fruits of memories of
Right and wrongs.
wrongs look like donkeys dragging the heavy cart
in the heart,
Rights are good enough to pay you a reward.
This garden waits for the endless time,
For the perfect canopy and the stint less sunshine.

3. Hopes

Pull the ropes of hopes,
Heavy hearts just soar.
Feel as light as feather,
That can change your weather.
glitches in your day make
you feel trolled.
But hopes catch you in
That cold,
Make you bold and warm
In the blanket old.
Be patient if you feel
Tightened in the round universe,
One day you sit and read
Your own stories on the
Sea shore.

4. Insane

Nowadays my words are trembling,
Cause I am very insane,
I love success but I am more afraid of
Failure pain.
Sometimes it feels like I am
Standing in the hail,
No umbrella, no tree for shade.
I try to be honest with myself,
But not Brave enough to count
the words.
The drops of courage in my mouth,
I am afraid when I get my crown.
Life is standing in disaster,
But nothing yet planned,
Screaming voices inside me
Hoarding,
But I just lost track.
I find this fear is immortal
In me like my grave,
Still, life takes place because
That universe always craves.

5. Story on repeat

My shallow feet are on concrete,
your delicate vanity stint less,
a heaven heart on the crumbled tracks
the dangling daffodils talk about
my rummage glories.
From the mad time to the bad time,
From being a frown to the crown,
In my smitten soul, there are
Many anecdotes but this one
Cling with my wagons of burning
Coal.
In the probability of finding chivalrous
Men for events of Esther life,
Walk across the deadly nightshade in the
Gardens of the chapel,
In the anonymous sounds of anklet.
Every night imaginary quartet sings my story
On repeat with songs and magical beat.

6. Melted hearts

Melted hearts in search of
nectar of flowers,
Butterfly in the blue sky with
their colourful Wings.
Both butterflies and flowers are
Sensitive and fragile,
So, they don't prefer to live in a crowd.
They spent their life in the meadow of solitude
And grace, in a calm place.
The fragile flowers and butterflies meet,
These were the meadows that are too
far from Streets,
In this meadow, grassy land is covered by
dandelions of love and daffodils of faith.
Ecstasy comes even on Sad face.
Business, an enormous powerful face,
They are not interested in this meadow and grace,
He is a stone-hearted giant that tramples
over flowers,
They Love crowds, they mostly stay in
markets for making legacy and profound.
They come into this meadow but,
Nothing change, his stone-heart
Just want a legacy to make.

He plucks the flowers and put them
For sale,
He catches all the butterflies and kept these
In cage.
Over the meadow, they do the construction of
Buildings and malls.
Now the meadow lost all those
magical butterfly and beautiful shiny flowers.
under the building,
there is a big graveyard of melted hearts with
wounds.
Melted hearts lost their solitary sounds.

7. Attic

over the wooden stage,

In an attic,

The crazy futile destiny

In my pocket.

Snow covered pitched roof

Of my sky parlor,

With hanging yellow bulbs

In the corners.

In the extreme ends, there

I am sitting in a frock frilled,

With an old witty box,

I start with my sweet little

Kitty, she's playing with

my Socks.

There is something mysterious

In that box,

When I open startled way with

My Pillow,

Playing and sputtering kitty sit

Resilient in a way,

I go over the bench and start

Smiling with clinging

My pillow over the head,

In the box there is beautiful scarf

I AM A POET

that sandy gift me,
When we are in love.
Our conversations may end but
The love in our hearts and scarf
stays.

8. Loop

Looking over the pictures of life,
Fresh sweet smearing like belladonna,
But these pink petals holding poison
But I just want to know what actually
Did I mean to be?
The question arrived at my door,
Who am I?
Where I am going?
My heart says the only thing I want
To hear is truth.
I say but I am a story and I have two
Sides,
I am really confused about which is my true side?
The heart thoroughly says you may have
Two sides, but truth has no angles.
I say every story has its angle and turning
Points.
My heart said that Is why you are confused
I say no with quiet breathing, but my heart
Explain that you are running in a loop,
And you will never be able to define yourself
Until you come to of this loop into the truth.

9. hollow talks

If you are feeling hollow, so might be
an empty vessel,
Your shape and size may vary but
your hollowness
Is similar to an empty heart,
A heart that cries over tunes of guitar,
One who plays with lonely beats and who
I don't even know how it feels to be
In infinity.
I know you are not okay,
Ending your day for someone else's
Life.
You don't define but you are a divine,
Your eulogy is bringing you sad prose.
You may be a cylindrical well
Dark and empty.
Eyes can't see your depth,
I wish I have the equipment to
Measure your emptiness and stress.
Never leave the ropes of hope,
But don't put yourself in the false
Hope.
Drop yourself into darkness and
Tell yourself all the truth.

Facing things can make your
Hollowness turns into a volume
then you have the strength from inside
now you are ready to ride this life.

10. Window

I remember a day, through the

Curtains of teapots printing,

From that window, I see a room

Full of mercy.

The glittery colourful lights,

Just like a fairy-tale night.

Outside the room there are

Huge trees in the woods.

Through the canopy darkness

Watching the lights,

With Colours red, green and blue.

The moment full of ecstasy,

frozen in time in room.

The floor dancing with balloons,

The ceiling with dangling windchime

And hanging bulbs are waving.

The doors are clinging with nail

In surprise,

When a girl standing with yellow

Lilies, and cheerful smile,

Boy enter with surprise,

There is beautiful pastel blueberry Cake

on the small skimpy wooden table,

with her smitten expression she gave

lilies to him,
there happy faces seem like the real
meaning of glory,
that was something magical,
that's how beautiful day end with this story

11. life that rhyme

I am the one on hold,
Your eyes are blocking my road,
Precious diamond with the necklace
Of gold.
Dad screaming at me for that wrong mould
Every day my life is getting old.
The season changes with increasing cold
I put my precious things on sold
So, life clings me on a rope
The letter to life is written in bold
There are few parts of life that I fold
That's why my life is untold.

12. lake of faith

How hell are the people
Who we thought are the best.
It is hard to accept, they have
Nothing adorable left.
With faith, the person looks like lord,
Without faith, it was the disgusting
Box of trepidation,
I am afraid to open it, maybe they are
Just fraud.
With faith, we even love to walk with
That person,
Without faith a disgusting reality
That we just wanted to forget.
In faith there is power,
nobody Can take it for granted.
this power has magical flames
it makes you follow the routes that
you never take.
Sometimes it is just a lake of
Disappointments,
Never give it easily to someone else
otherwise your life will have broken
peices that never good shape.

13. Simplicity

From the pool of expectation
to the leaves of the tree,
We try to fill our hearts with
Joy and greenery,
The scenery that we create
The feeling from our imagination
Is similar to the words of music that
I use to hear,
Sitting Under an oak tree gives
peace to the crowded soul which is
inflicting by the sting of a bee.
Now it is quite pretty that we are
Not similar like twins sitting over a twig.
The thing we have to keep in
Our sweetheart is politeness and
Simplicity.

14. Eulogy spaces

Belladonna grows near my wall old,
Near the pond, there are a lot of fish that flow,
Orchards blooming places for peace,
But I died suddenly.
No disease, I am not even panicking,
No heart attack, nothing at all.
my vanity disappears in a sea of chaos.
My husband took daffodils for my grave,
I am a patient lady calming down there
And listening to the last wishes people made.
Some say I am elegant and beautiful,
Some laughing over my death,
Some are nervous and panicked
But my husband treats me the best.
He took all the love letters,
I have written to him,
And crave over my grave,
I am happily reading them all
In the silence that never fades.

15. Wrong house

Roots are breaking me,
I don't know how much they
Are taking from me.
For solving this mystery,
I go back to history,
So, I go back home but
I just unfold another consistory.
I was tangled in a Rubik cube house,
If you try to match with one,
There is always another one who denies it.
It's tough to be an old child
Of home,
Though the house is the same but facts
about of home get changed.

16. Sew all dreams

When everyone trying to find out
My weak parts,
When they started creating my graveyard,
When life is running far and no one cares
About my homeless heart
I don't give up, I just run over them by
Crashing their waves.
I ran into my vitality.
The horrible dream sew into a beautiful
Reality.

17. Roots

Roots of a person are very clever,
They will tell how to treat others,
How to greet others.
Passionate heart and
responsible soul,
So many obstacles for
reaching the goal.
Adjourn the resumed talk,
Now you have dropped passion and
make yourself walk,
there is scrambling stint less road
ahead.
It is hard but you have to
become the Capitalist.
You now become the warrior
to those
Tenuous people whom you
are supporting.
By giving up on your dreams
you are running other's dreams,
In the form of money and resources.
You are the maker of this life wheel,
You become father and mother
Proud to be.

18. Ignorance

In the ignorance of life,
We try to pump air into the balloon life,
But one sharpy corner can take you to the end.
And when the Limit of the balloon comes like saturation of salt,
So, your graveyard becomes your immortal land,
Your husband comes over that land collect
to pieces of memories that you end,
in his arms with last breathe.
Travelling in this world is the last thing,
That she wishes, after death she realizes,
The meaning of flowers that her husband brings.
At that moment she reaches her eternity.
In her solitude, there is peace and bundles
Of memories,
Her sad prose was frozen under the snow
And the soul spending his parts with death
And solitude.

19. dampen wings

Sometimes helping turnout to mess,
Loving becomes walls of disrespect,
The person who cares gifts you stint less
Chaos,
You can't love daffodils anymore.
The dampened spirits are traversing your
Vigour soul,
Honesty honour has hidden humour hazy
Humble hands, for curing the wounds
On home.
My daisy divine has a mysterious
Cloth,
He wears that with an anklet and walks
On the resilient floor.
Now in this world, I need more blue sky
And the curtain of peace.
Because I think my dampen spirit need
To heal.

20. Irrational life

Reason has no season,
Burden bundles in my head
For no reason,
I like the rainy season but summer
And winter also have
interesting Vision.
The numbers are odd and
even,
But my life is irrational
like pageant.
Catching butterflies in the division.
I am on a very deadly mission,
That One day I am on television.

21. Calendar

the calendar with dates,
change the season with a maze,
but the changes they make,
make you feel amazed.
You have discovered,
The shades of soft sun,
The cold and freeze kind
Of breeze,
The rain pouring with a
Cup of tea.
The snowflakes are like a home
Covered with cotton with a
Snowman standing in it.
The smitten heart feeling
Raised,
The height and texture of
The plant has changed.
Within all that changes,
Everything changed but still
I am watching the clock and
Waiting for the same name.

22. Innocent

The closest we feel that far we are,
In the closet of life, feelings and emotion
Play the trad tunes on my guitar.
Our little heart doesn't know anything about
In reality, he uses to play with butterflies in the
Solitary garden of virtuality.
Is reality a good thing to accept?
Or ignorant happiness brings flowers?
Did we need to take them?
Sometimes I just feel like reality is craft
Of intelligence and we have to believe
Our Instinct, because realizing reality gives you
Freedom of vitality.
We have to solve both sides of the equation,
to know what you actually want to feel.
that's how we balance the equation of life
simply.

23. Grandma

The old eyes and old elbow
The old home and old laugh,
But family strengthens her
Every day to move even in
Scar.
Few things she keeps in her
Purse, that is emotion and
careless whispers.
her love of potato
And rice makes her energetic
And kind.
She also has some forms of
Art, how to convince the shopkeeper
To get a good bargain in grocery mart.
She also knows how to scold my aunt
Even her sharp ear may hear a whisper
That we sister talks at night.
Some people she hates and some
She likes, she knows everything but
She only uses to smile.

24. From the Outside

That some doors are locked forever,
Like the door of the graveyard.
I wish someone to find the key
And courage to open the door.
Otherwise, you also die without
Home.

25. My Graveyard

Waiting to have someone I
End time with,
Until life make me completely
Sleep,
If I never awoke again still I have
Smitten memories,
That crash on your breathe.
That always makes me feel
Alive like a story,
How beautiful my grave look
When you come for me with
Yellow lilies.
Just the green grass of solitude
In bird chirping and my love
Remembering me.

26. Artist

We all love the artist and their art,
We forgot that we don't even know who
They are?
We assume that a good artist must be
a good person,
and start having faith in them,
but beliefs and reality have a wide
gap that you can't fill,
you believe and you admire but
one day suddenly you meet them
and their reality,
Sometimes they make you feel better and inspireing
But many times, you don't like the way they are styling
And the Real colours they show,
This is how you meet reality and you grow
Otherwise, you lost in this world of illusion
And you even don't know.

27. Shady oak

We are like a shady oak tree,
give shelter even to an enemy.
The ecstatic aroma inside me,
Cue my mind to feel the solitude
And beauty.
The length of the tree defines
By its roots,
In the insidious world, roots are
Equally long as a tree.
Just like a parallel world of
Reflection, downside and deep.
Similarly, we all got cues and subconscious
things from the person parallel to thee.
This world looks futile and strained,
But actually, it is the umbrella of chaos holding
The bumblebee.
Roots give the texture and name to the
Tree, how sneak and gesture you have to
Give it to somebody.
Sometimes Parallel universe deep down
digging your Demon to make a frown.
You have to be resilient enough to survive in
Both worlds that cling to your noun.

28. Critical

Life is the name of confusions
That make us feel conscious,
Logical and emotional.
why life ask such questions?
that I can't able to answer.
Is life taking some kind of
Exam?
Or there is no accurate answer
Of these questions.
Answers have hidden
Questions,
That hold ocean of chaos,
They hold incredible future untold
And present problems
from which, You Are going through.
That need critical decision
Making And wisdom of knowledge.
But turmoil turning again
And again.
Brain is doing brainstorming again
And again,
And Soul passes through trepidation
Phase.
Frown trespassing in my mind,

That make me feel I am not fine.
There is no eraser to rub the
Decisions that were taken wrong,
Failure full of frown,
Give me anxiety crown.
There are tear in my eyes.
No more lesson needed to learn.
I think I am enough of being wise.
still failure following.
Now its decision time,
Destiny play with your mind
And you take decision when
Time comes,
It means life is all about
Confusions.

thank you

    for reading!!

9 798887 724188